Gracious House Keeping

Books by Mrs. White

For the Love of Christian Homemaking

Mother's Book of Home Economics

Living on His Income

Economy for the Christian Home

Mother's Hour

At Mother's House

Introduction to Home Economics

Early Morning Revival Challenge

Prentiss Study Deluxe Edition

Mother's Faith

Old Fashioned Motherhood

An Old Fashioned Budget

Homemaking for Happiness

(Cover photograph taken in Manchester, Vermont in 2019 by Mrs. Sharon White: Mrs. Robert Lincoln's upstairs parlour, at her summer mansion, built in 1905.)

Gracious House Keeping

Advice, Encouragement, and Cleaning Help
for the Christian Housewife

By Mrs. Sharon White

All Scripture Quotations are from the King James Bible.

Copyright 2022 by Mrs. Sharon White and The Legacy of Home Press:

.

ISBN Number: 978-1-956616-18-7

Gracious House Keeping: Advice, Encouragement, and Cleaning Help for the Christian Housewife

Author: Mrs. Sharon White

The Legacy of Home Press

Vermont - U.S.A.

Contents

Part 1

Part 2

~ This little book is full of old fashioned paintings of family and home life. These were originally published in the 1800's by Currier and Ives. May the illustrations bring you cheer and inspiration! ~

~ *Part 1*~

Encouragement

~ *Peace in the Home*~

"Peace be within thy walls…"

Psalm 122:7

"Thou wilt keep him in perfect peace, whose mind is stayed on thee: because he trusteth in thee."

Isaiah 26:3

"The Lord will give strength unto his people; the Lord will bless his people with peace."

Psalm 29:11

{Illustration on previous page: "Roses and Rosebuds," 1862 by Currier and Ives.}

~ *Chapter 1*~

HARVESTING.

{Illustration on previous page: "Harvesting," 1856 by Currier and Ives.}

~ Chapter 1~

Introduction

Is the art of housekeeping fading away? We are told that most women have stopped working full-time as homemakers. Children are growing up in families where, it seems, there isn't anyone at home. Who will be there to keep the home fires burning? Shouldn't there be a housewife always available to welcome and comfort family, guests, and those in need?

For the housewife of today, I want to encourage you in your efforts. Keeping house is a greatly needed occupation and I believe we just need a little encouragement and inspiration.

In this small book I will describe a basic routine for cleaning the house. There will be both a daily routine and a weekly routine to help maintain a lovely and tidy home. I will also share some ideas for those who are chronically ill, or who have trouble getting enough energy to do the work.

You may notice that I have not gone into much detail about getting children to help with chores. There is an important reason for this. Once a household is established, before the children arrive, and during the babyhood years, it is the housewife, herself, who manages the home almost entirely alone. Later, the children are given chores and they help with domestic care. All too soon, the children are grown and the beautiful art of *keeping house* is done just by the housewife. It is a joy and a blessing for this to be a life-long vocation. She is not just there to clean and cook. (Kitchen work is much easier these days and many husbands are also helping.) She is providing a respite of rest and a real old fashioned home with great love and care. House-keeping is about nurturing a lovely home with grace and goodness.

Once our cleaning foundation is settled, I will share the most important part of keeping house. This is what the house keeper does with her time. It includes her cheerfulness, the peace she creates, the work she does, her gentle frugality, and the culture she is providing for her loved ones. We will go over topics such as manners, making things look pretty, charitable efforts, setting up a work basket, and learning to enjoy the blessing of the honorable post you hold as House Keeper.

~ *Chapter 2*~

THE FOUR SEASONS OF LIFE: MIDDLE AGE.

{Illustration on previous page: "The Four Seasons of Life: Middle Age," 1869 by Currier and Ives.}

~ Chapter 2~

The Lived – in House Dilemma

We had been enjoying the beautiful summer season with all the rest and pleasantries of warm, happy days at home. The grandchildren were on vacation from school and were free to visit us as much as possible. We had some projects about the house and grounds for which we were kept busy during spare moments. Grown children and grandchildren visited us for many hours each day. They were our frequent and much welcomed guests. We were delighted with their company.

One morning we were brought to a sudden realization that our home was not as neat as we once thought. A little picture postcard had arrived in the mail. It was from the former owner of our house, an old neighbor who now lived out of state. She planned to visit the area, wrote down the dates she would be nearby, and said she hoped to see us. The first date of her vacation was the following day! We were happy with the prospect of seeing her and showing her around her old home. But when we looked about we realized our house had that "lived –in look" that is common in these days. We suddenly saw the rooms with new eyes. Would anyone understand why the corner of the couch was piled up with blankets? Why didn't someone put them away where they belonged? Would anyone think the bureau, in my bedroom, looked pretty with the piles of books and clutter that I had allowed to accumulate? What about the card table I had set up in one of the rooms? It held a stack of books, papers, and binder notebooks that I had carelessly laid out because of a writing project I had been working on. Why didn't I put things away after use, or organize them neatly when I was not actively engaged in the project? My kitchen table was not in order. My furniture needed a bit of polishing. Our home, I realized, looked like we had been quietly neglecting it! I shuddered.

There is a common phrase we use to excuse our lack of house keeping. We say our home is "lived-in." But doesn't this mean we are not taking care of it? On that summer morning, when we realized an elderly friend, from a completely different generation, would come for a visit, we had some mixed feelings. It was a dilemma. While we enjoyed having things laying about, or what one would say is "comfortable," it was not really an orderly or pleasant place to be. All this time I had thought my house was clean. But it didn't really meet our standards of a nice home, when we thought of an unexpected guest coming to see it!

It only took us a short time to get everything tidied up. We did a little dusting and vacuuming. I put things away that were on my bureau and card table. The couch was made neat and the extra blankets were put away. I laid out a fresh tablecloth on my kitchen table and straightened the chairs to create a pleasant look of rest and welcome. All of a sudden everything looked extra lovely. It looked like we loved our home and were taking care of it. We kept the house neat each day after that. It only takes a few minutes when there is order and routine in house keeping. This is something we must remember to do each day, not just because we might have unexpected company, but because it keeps things truly comfortable and restful to have lovely surroundings.

Now I want to ask you a question. If you received notice that someone was going to suddenly visit you, would your home be company ready? If not, how long would it take you to quickly tidy up? If we all have a routine in place, a sort of manual for keeping house, it will not take long to get things in order that have gone a little by the wayside.

In the following chapters I am going to give suggestions for both daily and weekly work that can lay a basic foundation for keeping a nice home. If we keep up with the daily work, things will not get too out of control in cases of illness, or a crisis. We should also find joy in the labor.

House Keeping is an art and worthy of our time and effort. Taking care of a home and a family is a much needed skill that should be cultivated and passed on throughout the generations. We need a pleasant place of rest and refuge. I hope you find encouragement and help in this little book.

~ *Chapter 3*~

FARM AND FIRESIDE.

{Illustration on previous page: "Farm and Fireside," 1878 by Currier and Ives.}

~ Chapter 3~

The Daily Work

When some of my grandchildren were very young, I remember spending hours in their little nursery room. They would toddle around and play while I kept watch over them. I would read stories, give them hugs, and enjoy their company. I would also do something onlookers might call, "playing house." I would tidy the room, organize the toys, set up pretty pillows on chairs, and place a nice blanket over the rocking chair. I would make sure the curtains were orderly and pretty.

When the children tired of their blocks, they would pick up another game or book while I reset the blocks in an inviting way. I might use them to build a little house, garage for the toy cars, or set them out by color and shape. Any arrangement that might look fun was set out for their happy time of play. Soon they would tire of their game, turn around and see the new display of blocks, and get excited to play with them again. At the end of each day, the nursery was put back in order and a wonderful new display was arranged for their delight the following morning. This reminds me of the joy of house keeping.

I have visited the homes of my grown children and enjoyed the little work of making things look extra pretty. If the table was not cleared from breakfast, I would clear and wash it off so it would look inviting for the family to have a tea break, draw pictures, or just sit and enjoy the pleasant room. This is homemaking. It is doing those little touches throughout the day, as a normal action, something like second-nature, or a habit of spreading the goodness of home whenever the need is presented.

Years ago, when I was a young mother, my husband took over making the coffee. I have always enjoyed tea and never liked the taste of coffee, so he was happy to make it himself. Whenever my mother visited us, she would do little touches of "home" in the kitchen or living room while we visited. This sweet habit of making things pleasant was something I've picked up from her example. When she saw a need, she would just automatically take care of it. She had the skill and training in home economics so it was normal for her to just do those little chores as she went about the day's routine.

One day, during her visit, she noticed our coffee pot needed a thorough cleaning. While I took care of the children and did some housework, she quickly cleaned the coffeemaker and made it look new again. I hardly noticed her doing this work, because we were visiting, talking, and busy. But later that evening, when my husband came home from work, he went to make a pot of coffee. He turned to look at me and said, "Was your mother here today?" I love that he immediately noticed and knew my dear mother had done this kind service. Making a home look nice and pleasant are good deeds.

The daily work includes simple chores that we are all familiar with. We make the meals and we clean up after them. We do the dishes, wash the table and counters, and sweep the floors. We make the beds and keep everything sanitary and orderly. In general, we simply clean up after ourselves and keep the home looking neat and presentable. It is a labor of love and service which takes time and effort. We need not rush or stress. Try to go at a slower pace. Have you ever made a batch of bread dough by first measuring and *sifting* the flour? It is a quiet, peaceful work that is enjoyable when we realize all work happens amidst the interruptions and trouble of the day.

We do the work of service with good manners, kindness, and a sense of duty. This is similar to being professional in one's vocation. We do good work and we do it in a beautiful way. *Slow down the chores*. Make homemaking look pretty. Stay cheerful.

Are you rushing about always trying to get the next mess cleaned? Are you stressed out because the messes keep happening? Try to keep in mind that the messes are normal and there are little rules we can set up to prevent unnecessary disorder. Some may have a rule that the family only eats in the dining room. In this way, one is not constantly vacuuming up crumbs all over the house. Another idea is to keep toys and crayons off the kitchen table unless the table has already been washed, dried, and cleared of snacks or meals. In other words, don't mix food and beverages with playing or doing paperwork. This will prevent spills and messes from getting on the papers or toys. It makes cleaning easier. Each home may have their own ways of preventing disasters by setting up rules that work for them.

Do you have trouble getting the strength and energy to do the daily work? Here is a possible solution. ***Do ten things***. In addition to the cooking and cleaning up after three meals each day, do five things in the morning and five things in the afternoon. This breaks up the work and will even help with your health. The work, the labor, is like exercise and something we all need to do each day.

Some ideas for the ten things may include: Dusting, vacuuming, organizing paperwork, cleaning up a stack of clutter, washing mirrors, changing bed sheets, cleaning out a purse, or washing the dish drainer. Each item does not take very long but will help keep the house looking nice.

If you are suffering from chronic illness, doing these little jobs, spread out throughout the day, will brighten your mood as well as your home. Try to do some walking each day to increase your strength and energy. Be as productive as you can. Just rest as much as possible between each task.

I remember the last year of my mother's life when she was a widow, living on her own. She had chronic health issues and a heart condition. She walked with a cane, but somehow she managed to do a little work throughout the day to keep her home looking clean and pleasant.

We will always find something to do with our time. Just consider little jobs you can do that will add up, at the end of each day, to make your home lovely. The work is worth the effort it cost.

~ *Chapter 4*~

HOME TO THANKSGIVING.

{Illustration on previous page: "Home to Thanksgiving," 1867 by Currier and Ives.}

~ Chapter 4~

The Five Day Homemaking Plan

I was in the hospital a couple of weeks ago. When I got home, I needed my family to help with the cleaning and cooking. I was served meals in bed and was able to rest and recover. After a few days, I was able to do small tasks, such as paying a bill, getting my own tea, and making toast. Each little job wore me out and I had to rest. Soon I was thinking about housekeeping. I wanted to do some extra work in our front parlour. My plan was to take down all the curtains and get them washed. I told my husband what I had hoped to do, while I rested on the couch. He smiled. "Only if you are able," he cautioned. I knew he was right, and thought it would have to wait until I felt well enough. However, to my surprise, he started taking down all the curtains for me. All I had to do was load them in the washing machine.

Throughout that entire day, I rested, then worked, then rested again. During that morning, I dusted some of the furniture. I had to recover from that bit of labor and went to lay down. Later, I was able to finish the dusting. I pulled out the vacuum cleaner. It sat on the living room floor, by the table, until late that afternoon. It took me that long to get enough energy. I placed a pile of clutter, from on top of my hutch, onto the floor in my bedroom. I would get to that later, I told myself. By lunch - time, the curtains were all washed and clean. I called downstairs to my husband, "the curtains are ready." He sweetly came to my rescue and, after I laid them out for him, they were put back on all the windows. It was getting dark. I still had not put a fresh tablecloth on the table. I also wanted to clear off the sideboard table and make it pretty. Just after dinner, I was able to do those last little jobs. The parlour looked lovely and was fresh and clean. I had worked hard, but also, somehow, spent most of the day in bed. I noticed the pile of clutter on my bedroom floor. I did not know if I could sort it all. It seemed overwhelming. But after another long hour of rest, I was ready to sit on the floor and separate it all in piles. I was surprised how quickly the job was finished. I tossed catalogs in the recycling, sorted papers and put them into folders in the filing cabinet, and saved the catalogs I wanted to keep, putting them in a cabinet. All was finished. This type of housekeeping is very common for those who are struggling with an illness or are trying to regain their strength. The pleasant work of making home beautiful is done amidst the difficulties of life. Whether it is sickness, interruptions, or the usual needs of the family, the labor can be accomplished by doing a little, here – and - there, throughout the day.

I have found by giving each day of the week a certain duty, it is easier to keep up with the work.

Here is the plan:

Monday – Organize and Budget.

Tuesday – Laundry and Mending, Ironing and Sewing.

Wednesday – Deep Cleaning.

Thursday – Errands and Shopping.

Friday – Cooking and Baking.

I will go into a little more detail for each week day. Please note: There are no assigned duties for Saturday and Sunday, other than the normal work that must be done each day.

Monday

It is easy for our homes to be overcome with clutter. The table might have a stack of mail, or paperwork, that has not been put away. Chairs might hold unfolded laundry. Shoes might be in a pile near the door. Books might be in disorder in a bookcase. The bureau might be piled with things we have not had a chance to put away. All these things can lead to a messy home. On Mondays we can decide to do the organizing. We can sort and put everything away. We can rearrange the bookcase, making it neat. We can make the shoes and coats look orderly. The stack of papers can be filed or tossed. It is a good day to go over the written budget, see what bills have been paid, and handle any necessary correspondence or phone calls. We decide to make the day about organizing and this will help maintain the home.

Tuesday

This is a good day to do the laundry. In some homes, especially when there are small children, laundry is often done on a daily basis. On Tuesday we can have a special focus on laundry to make sure the towels, washcloths, and bedding is clean.

We can do any necessary ironing, which is an old time, peaceful work. It may even be a good opportunity, if one has an interest, to set up a sewing project. It is good to check the condition of our clothing. It is also a day for mending. We can fix a rip on the lining of a coat. We can replace missing buttons. We can sew the fray on a skirt hem. It is also a good day to notice if any clothing needs to be discarded. We can tidy up the bureau drawers and closets.

It is also important to wash the bed sheets. I want to mention something about flat sheets. The use of them seems to have gone out of fashion in the younger generation of homes. May I mention why they are important? First, we have the fitted sheet, which covers the mattress. Next we put on the flat sheet. One sleeps between these two sheets, which are washed each week.

They keep the bed fresh and clean. It is not so common to wash the comforters and blankets that are on top of the flat sheet. This is why the flat sheet helps keep the other blankets clean. It is very comforting, especially for a child, to get into a cozy, clean bed for a good night sleep.

Keep the beds nicely made, with the blankets tucked in, and the comforter neatly arrayed. Be sure to fold and put away the laundry, as the loads of washing are completed, throughout the day.

Wednesday

This is the day for the heavy work. It should take about 2 hours, depending on the size of your home. It is the day for deep cleaning. I have included a chart in Part 2 to make it easy to see all the possible jobs one might want to do on this day. Mostly the day includes washing floors, cleaning bathrooms, dusting, vacuuming, etc. I used to be able to do all this work in one block of time. However, it is harder when there is much going on at home. When I have children or grandchildren, I can get some helpers. But when I have to do the work on my own, I take many breaks. But the actual 2 hours of work, means that I might do a half hour at a time, or perhaps an hour in the morning and the last hour in the afternoon. It is also perfectly okay if the work takes longer as well.

Thursday

If we can avoid going to the store too often, we can save both energy and money. We can choose Thursday as our day for errands and shopping. With this weekly routine in place, we can plan in advance in order to save gas and time. I usually go to the bank and post office on errand day. After I do the grocery shopping, I often stop and visit at the home of one of my grown children, before heading back to my own house. It takes a lot of energy to do the shopping. It is always nice to get back home, get everything put away, and then take a break. I am usually home in time for lunch and have time for a good rest.

Friday

This is a good day to do any last minute preparations for the weekend. I have often premade a lasagna, which is easy to bake and serve for the next day. I just mix all the ingredients together, layering them in a large pan, and then cover it, without baking, to store in the refrigerator. When we are ready, it is easy to take off the cover and just bake it for dinner, with extra left - over for the next day. It might be a nice time to bake cookies or brownies as a special treat. When I had a house full of young children, I would bake bread, every Friday, which we all enjoyed. These special times of cooking and baking help make the weekend pleasant.

You can set your work for any day that works best for you. It is also common to do many of these chores any day as needed. The purpose of the routine, for each assigned day, is so that we have a focus to accomplish certain tasks on a regular basis. It is less overwhelming when we have a plan.

~ *Chapter 5*~

A MANSION OF THE OLDEN TIME.

{Illustration on previous page: "A Mansion of the Olden Time," 1856 by Currier and Ives.}

~ *Chapter 5*~

Restful Weekends

The home is organized. It has been dusted and cleaned. Some food has been prepared in advance to make the weekend easier. We have worked hard all week, keeping a nice home, and now we can really enjoy happy days with the family.

We want home to be inviting. We want it to be pleasant. It ought to be the place we all want to spend our time, more than anywhere else. It should be a place of peace, where the family bonds and enjoys each other's company.

Here are some ideas for enjoying the weekends at home:

Simple Amusements

The center of the living room was often an old piano. All in the family would play for fun, whether they had formal lessons or not. Children, in particular, love to just play around with the keys. A bench, by the piano, holds music books, hymnals, Christmas carols, and instruction books. The family is free to choose from this selection for practice or for fun. There are beginner books which show exactly how to play simple Christmas songs, such as "Jingle Bells," which are fun for anyone, young or old, to be able to play something without knowing how to read music.

One of my grown children recently acquired a beautiful old piano for free. It has not been "tuned" as we have been told, but that doesn't matter to any of us. Nearly every visitor that stops by is drawn to that piano and enjoys sitting on the bench and just playing for fun.

A home with art supplies is a blessing. If there are drawing pencils, assorted paper, crayons, watercolor paints and such, anyone can sit down at the table and enjoy a time of creativity.

It is nice to have board games stored in a cabinet or bookcase. The most common games to have include: Checkers, Chess, Boggle, Scrabble, Battleship, Connect Four, and Monopoly. These are all classic and enjoyable for both young and old.

Enjoying the Outdoors

It is lovely to have a well - kept yard. Perhaps there are flowers to pick and enjoy. Maybe there is a walking path on larger estates where one can just get fresh air and a bit of wonderful exercise on the grounds of home. Some homes have patio furniture, lawn chairs, or park benches for a time of outdoor rest. When the property is smaller, there may be little flower beds and gardens to nurture and tend. One can have picnics on the lawn, which is a restful and pleasant part of being at home. In winter, walks in the snow, all bundled up, are lovely forms of recreation amidst the beauty of nature.

Whether the yard is elaborately landscaped or a work- in-progress, any bit of effort, each week, will help bond the family as they work together with plans and little jobs to keep it looking pleasant.

I want to mention that there are times when we cannot maintain our yards. One year, in particular, due to a disabling injury, my husband was not able to take care of our property. It rarely was mowed. It would have looked entirely neglected, but for the blessing of beautiful wildflowers which had been planted throughout certain areas of the property. They gave it a shabby but lovely look, which we enjoyed until we were able to start keeping things nice again.

The Church

I will always have fond memories of getting ready for church. My Mother and Father would get all dressed up in their best clothes. We each had our own Bibles that we would bring with us. We would have a simple breakfast and then head out to the wonderful service. We attended 3 services and then a mid-week Bible Study. Some of us were in the choir and were part of the nursing home ministry. This was where our social life was centered – both in the church and in the home.

Our house was neat and clean so that when we returned, we would come home to pretty things. This boosts the mood, gives one a sense of contentment, and helps unite the family in a common bond of interests. My parents loved these things, and because they involved us and shared this with us, we loved them too. It was the love of home, of family, and of church. When we take care of the things we love, in active service, we are doing good deeds, which make things last.

The Ending of the Weekend

On Sunday evenings, it is a good time to prepare for the coming week. The rooms are tidied and put in order. There may be a dimness of lamplight as a signal to wind down the day. A simple supper is served at the table, we hear a prayer of thanksgiving from one of the family. Then we enjoy the fellowship of homemade food prepared with love.

Soon the kitchen is cleaned and everyone is getting ready for bed. There is a time of evening prayers and Bible reading. Then all are tucked into clean and cozy beds to get a good rest, remembering a wonderful weekend at home with the family.

~ *Chapter 6*~

FAMILY DEVOTION.

{Illustration on previous page: "Family Devotion," 1871 by Currier and Ives.}

~ Chapter 6~

Manners in the Home

We need a constant reminder of good etiquette. Good behavior is an example to all, showing that everyone is important and deserves kindness. In every family, there will be moods to contend with, troubles, mistakes, and disagreements. It is important to offer grace with a sense of compassion. We want our homes to be a haven of refuge. We want it to be full of forgiveness, patience, and love. This requires manners.

Here are some ideas for encouraging good manners in the home:

Special Words

There are some special words that ought to be spoken on a daily basis. We should say "please" whenever we ask for something, even if we are asking a child or an elderly adult. We should always say "thank you" when something is done for us. We should say, "I'm sorry" when we make a mistake, or when we accidentally cause someone harm. Another phrase, which will make others feel special is to say, with gentle sincerity, "I love you," or "you are loved."

Available for Service

Be willing to help others. We do not want to be selfish or too caught up in our own projects that we are not available for our family. When someone walks into your room, do you willingly say something like, "is there anything I can do for you?" This shows that others are important; that they are valuable and loved. Acts of service, done with cheerful willingness, is what a gracious house keeper is known for.

Take Care of Your Things

It is bad manners to leave a mess that someone else will trip over. It is not nice to leave clutter all over the house for someone else to clean up. To be kind and pleasant, we must pick up after ourselves. We should also help young children do this. Little ones learn by example. They do not naturally understand this need. We ought to come alongside them and say, "I will help you clean up your mess." Soon the child will learn this wonderful skill and start doing it on his own. But it takes time and effort. Maturity does not happen in a day. If this habit is started young, by the time the child is 8 years old, they often take care of their own things, with kind reminders when necessary.

Praise and Appreciation

It is important to encourage others in goodness. Tell them they have done a good job. Thank them for their help. Be sure they feel loved and appreciated. We need to be the cheerleaders of the home.

Spreading a Light of Goodness

We need to build the bonds of integrity and love. Reward the good you see with thanksgiving and warmth. Be an example of gracious kindness, with genuine smiles and joy. This is contagious. Guard your mood by focusing on the beauty of singing hymns, reading Psalms, saying precious prayers, and seeking the love of a close walk with the Lord. This will bring you peace. It will spread a light of goodness to those around you. This ongoing work cultivates a happy home.

~ *Chapter 7*~

{Illustration on previous page: "Winter in the Country," 1863 by Currier and Ives.}

~ Chapter 7~

Make Home Life Pretty

It is a snowy November day as I write this. There is a nice fire in our wood pellet stove. I have a drying rack covered with laundry, near the heat of the stove. The room is neatly in order. Soon I will put away the clothes. As I look through the curtains, I can see a blanket of whiteness all over the front property. I feel cozy and grateful for the beauty of home.

I love to see a comfortable home with pleasant surroundings. This helps keep us all cheerful. When we take the time to do our daily work, with genuine love and attention, our surroundings will be peaceful, calm, and enjoyable.

Here are some ideas that may help:

Dress Nicely

If the house keeper looks her prettiest, it sets the mood for a lovely home. We can wear house dresses, or something that is comfortable, yet attractive. There are pretty things that are also practical. We want to be able to work easily in what we are wearing, but also look lovely. There is a gentleness and a beauty to keeping house when one takes the time to choose nice items to wear.

Decorate with Grace

If we live in a humble home, even with little funds, we can still find a way to make it look charming. It may take years to acquire beautiful, yet inexpensive, paintings for the walls. Sometimes we inherit decorations that would fit in beautifully with our surroundings. At other times it is just as lovely to make delicate, homemade mottoes with such sayings as Bible verses or messages of love and welcome. These may end up being treasures that add to the beauty of the rooms. When we have pretty things to look at, we enjoy home more.

Keep Messes in Order

There are always going to be little messes in some of the rooms. Children may be busy with projects at the table or on the living room floor. These are normal and happy things to see. We want the family to enjoy their play. Still, when they are finished, they ought to be encouraged to put their things away, to clean up after themselves. If an ongoing project cannot easily be put away, at least make that mess look neat, stacked nicely, or just simply tidied and safely out of the way. Even small messes will not take away from the beauty of home as long as they are kept neatly aside.

Acts of Courtesy

When we are kind and pleasant to those of the household, we make homemaking look pretty. When we do our daily work with dignity and honor, we show the work as being profitable and noble. Our daily acts of kindness, with love and patience, brings about a gentleness which will gladden the heart.

The home can be our greatest project. It can be a work of art to create an atmosphere of beauty and grace. Our effort at bringing happiness and comfort to the family, and visitors, is a blessing. This makes home a pretty place to be.

~ *Chapter 8*~

{Illustration on previous page: "Winter Morning in the Country," 1873 by Currier and Ives.}

~ Chapter 8~

The Work Basket

It used to be common to sit and visit in the parlour with a work basket. Ladies would have mending and projects to do while they rested. When others expected to spend some time visiting, they would bring their own work basket from home. It was a lovely way to accomplish important things while enjoying the fellowship of others. While we may not have an actual basket full of work, we can easily find some projects to do with a nearby sewing box.

Very often, when I visit some of my grandchildren, I will bring my sewing box. They will give me any toys that need fixing. These are usually little stuffed bears or little toys with a cotton filling. I get my sewing needle ready and sew up the rips while I talk with the children. Soon their toys are back in order. The children enjoy looking for the spot where the toy was mended. They admire the work.

Some time ago, I noticed one of the younger boys had a hole in the knee of his play clothes. When he changed into something else, I offered to wash and mend them here at my house. My husband kindly gave me one of his nice, older shirts that he no longer needed. It had a thick, warm material in a color that nicely matched the pants. I measured and cut out a square and was soon busy sewing it on, covering the hole in the knee. I am no expert seamstress but do very basic work. I was delighted to see how nice the pants turned out. It looked almost stylish to have the quality patch, in just the right place, to match the pants.

Some years ago, my parents had a beautiful homemade quilt on their bed. After long use, the stitches were coming out of some of the squares, revealing cotton filling underneath. I spent part of an afternoon, with my sewing box handy, quietly mending each square until it was all tight and back in order.

Sometimes when I am on the telephone, with one of my grown children, I will be working on some sewing project. It is easy to just quietly stitch the hem on a homemade cloth napkin while I talk. I find that I am not in a rush to go do some work, and am much happier visiting while I am sewing or mending during the conversation.

When some of the grandchildren are here for the day, they get all of my attention. Yet, as we sit and talk, read stories, and just be together, I like to have some mending or sewing to work on as I rest on the couch. On one of their visits I got my winter coat and hand-stitched up some long neglected rips in the seam of the lining. The children laughed and talked to me while I sat and worked. It was so restful to just fix things while we enjoyed each other's company.

Sewing and mending is a quiet service that is much needed. It is a work of love and basic skill that blesses the family. It is also a pleasant way to enjoy our moments of rest.

~ *Chapter 9*~

PEACE AND PLENTY.

{Illustration on previous page: "Peace and Plenty," 1871 by Currier and Ives.}

~ Chapter 9~

Hand - Sewing Projects

I like to have some special project to work on. If there is no mending to do, I find it restful to work on a little hand-sewing. I will share a few ideas for those who might find this interesting. First, however, I want to say that sewing by hand just means that we thread a simple needle and do a basic stitch. We are not using a machine. I have a little sewing basket that was given to me by an aunt, many years ago, when I was a young girl. It has been frequently used all these years. It is one of my favorite things to have here at home.

Here are some easy project ideas:

Little Pouch

When I first taught my children to sew, we always started with a pouch. I would have them cut out one piece of scrap fabric. It measured around 8 inches by 4 inches. I would show them the difference between right sides (the pretty side which showed on the outside) and wrong sides (the duller side which was considered inside-out). I would say that, when we are sewing, we do "right sides together." In this way, we are sewing the inside- out part. I would have them fold the fabric in half. I taught them how to thread the needle with a knot at the end so the stitches would stay in place. I cut out a duplicate piece of fabric and would sew, as a demonstration, so we were doing the same project together, at the same time. We would just do a simple stitch, back and forth, until two sides were stitched together. The bottom of the pouch did not need to be stitched because it had been folded. Then we turned the top part down two little times, folding it under, so the edges of the fabric did not show. Then we pinned it in place and carefully sewed this "hem," all around the top. Once this was finished, the pouch was complete! The children worked on pouches over and over until they became very good at simple sewing. Once that was finished, they could make just about anything they wanted by hand, without help.

Homemade Cloth Napkins

I like to pick out a pretty floral fabric and use it to make simple cloth napkins. These are small, measuring around 10 inches by 14 inches. Once these pieces are cut out, I iron them, and then fold down the sides, just a bit, for little hems. These are then pinned and set aside until I have a chance to start sewing them. This is the easiest project to do that creates something useful and beautiful for the service of home.

Decorative Pillow Case

I have a small, decorative pillow on our parlour couch. It measures around 16 inches by 16 inches. It is plain with a solid color of blue. I decided to make a pillow case. It is far easier to regularly wash a pillow case, to keep it fresh and nice, rather than washing the pillow itself. I used the pillow for my pattern. I selected a beautiful, delicate floral fabric. My tools included a piece of chalk and a ruler to draw the lines for cutting. I made the pattern about 2 inches, all around, larger than the pillow itself. I used the same method as I use for making a pouch. The fabric was already folded over in half, before I cut it, so the bottom half did not need to be sewed. I only had to sew the two sides together and then do a little hem for the opening at the top. The finished project is lovely.

Basic Quilt

One of my grown daughters asked me to make her a homemade quilt for her home. She wanted some nice homemade things around. I make a simple, plain quilt, sewing by hand. When I made one of my first quilts, I made a little one for a doll for one of my children. I selected one piece of fabric. I then cut this up into about 9 squares. Then I sewed 3 squares together in a row. I did this for two more rows. Then I sewed each row together. I hemmed it all around and did not include any cotton inside or even a backing. Now I can do this for a larger quilt. I use a different fabric for the back, but do not include any cotton filling. It is just an old fashioned, plain quilt. For my daughter's quilt, I spent the first day picking out the fabric from what I had on hand. There were several different floral fabrics I was able to use. I took a piece of scrap fabric and, along with chalk and a ruler, cut out what I would use as my pattern piece. It was about 4 and one fourth inches by 5 and three fourth inches in size. I used this pattern piece to cut all the pieces I wanted for the finished quilt. I mixed up the different fabric squares to form some sort of order that appealed to me, and laid this out on the living room floor. These were then pinned together in rows, waiting for me to sew them, as I had time. I stored these on a card table, stacked neatly in the order I wanted to sew them. Once the pieces were all sewn together, I cut out a pretty piece of fabric to fit the entire back side of the quilt. I then folded the sides over and neatly sewed it in place. I took my time with this quilt, sewing whenever I sat in the parlour. I quietly and peacefully worked, at my leisure, as a form of pleasant recreation. At this pace, it took me about 9 months to finish the project. (I will include a very basic pattern for this in Part 2.)

Whatever time you can spend on little hand-sewing projects will be a blessing to the entire family. The more you practice, the more skilled you will become.

I have made little dresses, by hand, as well as aprons. I find it relaxing to sew by hand, rather than using a machine. If one can acquire the skill of basic sewing, one can mend or make just about anything. It also produces a beautiful sense of patience when one takes the time to slowly make something pretty.

~ *Chapter 10*~

EARLY WINTER.

{Illustration on previous page: "Early Winter," 1869 by Currier and Ives.}

~ Chapter 10~

Charitable Service

Is there money available, in your household budget, for good deeds? A great deal of money is often spent on the home. We may buy furniture, paint, carpets, curtains, kitchen-ware, and much more. We also spend money on food and clothing, as well as the cost of home repairs, monthly payments of rent or mortgage and the cost of our utilities. Some even spend money on elaborate entertaining. Keeping a house can be very expensive if one lives extravagantly. However, if one lives in a humbler manner, using gentle frugality, there will be money left over to save and to give away. There will be money available for good works.

It is a lovely feeling to have the basic expenses as low as possible. (Keep in mind: We are not being "cheap." It just means we are not wasteful or frivolous.) Knowing the simple bills are paid each month, that there is food in the pantry, and that the home is safe and comfortable gives one a sense of gratefulness. Living in a quiet, thrifty way, generally leads to a surplus of funds. This is gentle frugality.

When someone calls with a need of help, there is extra food available to share. There is even some money to help along in hard times. In the case of illness, the loss of a job, or some other crisis, a family will be in need. If we can relieve a bit of this suffering, with a kind gift to encourage, and lift others through their trouble, it is a blessing to them and to us.

Old time families, of modest means, were very careful with all the money that came into their home. They would give a portion to the church, and then put some aside for an emergency. They lived simply and were content and happy with little. These families often had a joyful Mother who made their days beautiful with her cheerful attitude and her creative skills in making a home, despite few resources. She would keep a clean and pretty house, prepare simple meals and serve them with love and beauty. The children were dearly loved and she was devoted to them. This way of simple, godly living is in great contrast to what many call the ways of the "idle rich." There have always been some who have great wealth but do not take care of it. They spend a great deal of their money and their time doing that which profits little. In the old days, people would spend many years building up their "life savings." In other words, they had a habit of saving all of their lives. If this is passed on to the next generation, it should be used wisely and carefully. However, if it falls into hands that are idle and wasteful, the result is that the entire life savings will be gone. It is important that every homemaker learns the skill of domestic economy. The careful and wise use of money is essential to every single home. For the peace and happiness of the family, we must learn to be content with little. In this way, it is a wonderful treat when we can acquire a few little things, over time, to brighten life at home. There is also a great joy in knowing there is money available to help those in need.

Giving a portion of our time and money to the poor is like a thank offering. It is a good deed which brings joy to the heart.

Be sure to pray over each need as it is presented. It is wonderful to work through your local church under solid guidance, with the deacons, for helping church members and the community.

I have found the works of charity to be one of the most pleasant aspects of homemaking. It is a precious labor - to bring comfort and help to others. It is like shining a light of cheer and encouragement. It is a beautiful and kind way to live. A life committed to charitable service is made possible by being a gracious and careful house keeper.

~ *Chapter 11~*

THE DAY OF REST.

{Illustration on previous page: "The Day of Rest," 1869 by Currier and Ives.}

~ Chapter 11~

A Real Old Fashioned Home

A few years ago I visited a museum of someone's home. It was a beautiful place. There were comfortable guest rooms, a beautiful dining room, parlours, a library, and bedrooms belonging to the family. The grounds were very peaceful on some acres of land. It was like going to see a retreat but was actually the home of a real family, from many years ago. This museum is in Manchester, Vermont. It is the summer home of Mr. and Mrs. Robert Lincoln. It was built in the early 1900's. (You can see Mrs. Lincoln's lovely private parlour on the front cover of this book.)

What I found particularly fascinating was to see how the family lived. There were bookcases in nearly every room, indicating that reading was a common pastime. There was more than one piano in the house. This showed that they enjoyed playing the piano as well as singing together. The library, on the first floor, was mostly used by Mr. Lincoln. He had comfortable chairs, a sturdy desk, and many books for his use. The windows all around the room showed a view of the beauty of nature. In a day when there were no computers, televisions, or cell phones, it is clear to see that he spent his time enjoying his surroundings and his family and guests. He also used that room to do some of his work.

In the upstairs parlour, there was a set of lovely pink sofas. The lamps were charming and set out for the comfort and happiness of those who were enjoying the room. The parlour contained a piano and a large writing desk. This was where the lady of the house wrote out her correspondence, did her embroidery, and enjoyed the piano. Her family, as well as any guests she was entertaining, spent time with her in this charming room. She had an incredible view, through the large windows, of the back grounds of the estate. The landscape included stunning mountains, carefully manicured hedges, and an abundant flower garden.

The family was called to meals in the dining room. This was a bright, beautifully decorated room with a formal table and impressive furnishings. An open door to the butler's pantry revealed an old time telephone. In those days, not a single person in the family would use the telephone. It was intended for the staff, or butler, to take any messages that were needed for the household. What a quiet and peaceful home that must have been! Clearly this was a place of wealth. However, their way of home-life is still considered ideal and common.

There are other museums, here in the United States, which show humbler means. I saw one which had pretty homemade curtains on the windows. There were homemade quilts on the beds. There was a rocking chair by the fireplace. The kitchen table was simply made but served a wonderful purpose for the family. There was a Bible prominently displayed which was a comfort to the family, bringing a light on their path. I can imagine them singing hymns by the cozy fireplace, content and thankful for one another.

In either case, family life was centered around the home. This was where they spent most of their time. Home gardens provided much of the food. There was work to do to keep things looking nice and the family housed and fed. This helped bond the family together in mutual love and interests.

Today, a real old fashioned home can be cultivated with the help of Mother. If she is joyful and cheerful in serving the family, it will bless those around her. She can take good care of the rooms, the laundry, the kitchen, and keep things looking cheerful and pretty. Her gracious manners, her kind deeds, her willingness to do the daily work, and her peaceful hospitality will help, every day of her life, to make a pleasant home. It is a precious work to be a house keeper.

~ *Part 2*~

Work Charts

~ Grace and Mercy in the Home~

"I will sing of the mercies of the Lord for ever: with my mouth will I make known thy faithfulness to all generations." - *Psalm 89:1*

"For thou, Lord, art good, and ready to forgive; and plenteous in mercy unto all them that call upon thee."

- Psalm 86:5

"But thou, O Lord, art a God full of compassion, and gracious, longsuffering, and plenteous in mercy and truth." - *Psalm 86:15*

"Be ye therefore merciful, as your Father also is merciful." - *Luke 6:36*

{Illustration on previous page: "Roses and Rosebuds," 1862 by Currier and Ives.}

Contents

The Beauty of Contentment

{ Illustration: "Roses and Rosebuds," 1862, Currier and Ives. }

"Not that I speak in respect of want: for I have learned, in whatsoever state I am, therewith to be content."

Philippians 4:11

~ Section 1~

Daily Work Routine

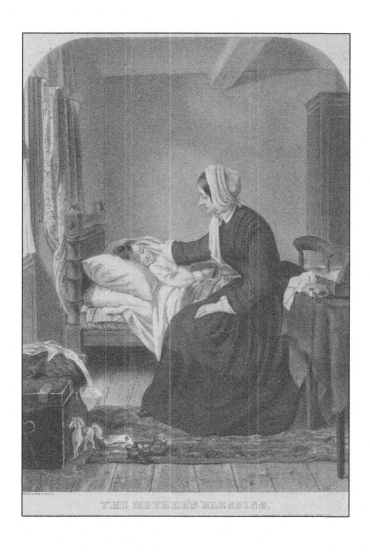

THE MOTHER'S BLESSING.

{Illustration on previous page: "The Mother's Blessing," 1856 by Currier and Ives.}

Morning –

Open the curtains and shades.

Make beds.

Prepare Breakfast.

Clean Kitchen.

Do Dishes.

Sweep Floors.

Open Windows to get fresh air into the rooms.

Put out clean towels and washcloths.

Start the scheduled work for the day of the week.

Afternoon –

Prepare Lunch.

Clean Kitchen.

Do Dishes.

Sweep Floors.

Check supplies: Fill the liquid hand-soap dispenser. Make sure there is soap, shampoo, etc. available for the day.

Tie up any trash. Put in fresh trash bags.

Be sure the bathroom is kept clean and in order.

Do any necessary dusting and polishing.

Evening –

Prepare Dinner.

Clean Kitchen.

Do Dishes.

Sweep Floors.

Close the curtains and shades.

Straighten chairs. Make sure rooms are in order, neat and ready for the next morning.

Be sure the dining room table is cleared off. Put out a nice tablecloth, neatly arranged, ready for tomorrow's breakfast.

Hospitality –

Welcome any Visitors.

Provide Refreshments.

Be sure they are Comfortable and Rested.

~ Section 2~

The Housekeeping Schedule

ROADSIDE COTTAGE.

{Illustration on previous page: "Roadside Cottage," 1856 by Currier and Ives.}

Monday -

Organize paperwork and books, put away clutter, handle correspondence, work on budget and bills.

Tuesday-

Laundry, Iron, Wash, Sew, Mend, Sort and organize Clothes, Change Bed-sheets.

Wednesday-

Deep clean house, 2 hours.

Thursday -

Errands, shopping, visiting.

Friday -

Cooking and Baking for weekend.

A Clean Heart

{ Illustration: "Roses and Rosebuds," 1862, Currier and Ives. }

"Create in me a clean heart, O God; and renew a right spirit within me."

Psalm 51:10

~ Section 3~

House Cleaning Wednesday

HOME SWEET HOME.

{Illustration on previous page: "Home Sweet Home," 1856 by Currier and Ives.}

Kitchen –

Wipe down all appliances.

Deep clean counters.

Scrub sink.

Clean inside of refrigerator.

Clean Microwave.

Clean Toaster Oven.

Sweep and Wash floor.

Bedrooms –

Dust.

Make Beds.

Wipe down windowsills.

Clean Mirror.

Vacuum.

Bathroom-

Scrub counters and shelves.

Clean mirror.

Scrub sink.

Scrub Bathtub.

Clean toilet.

Sweep and Wash floor.

Living room-

Dust all furniture and baseboards.

Vacuum carpet.

Clean windows and window sills.

Staircase and hallways -

Sweep and Vacuum.

Remove cobwebs.

Clean banisters.

Additional –

Wash Windows and dust Window sills.

Clean baseboards.

Remove any cobwebs on walls or ceilings.

Clean entryways.

Dust paintings and picture frames.

~ Section 4~

Basic Quilt Pattern

{Illustration on previous page: "Rustic Basket," 1856 by Currier and Ives.}

Homemade Quilt –

Cut squares 4 ¼ inches by 5 ¾ inches.

You will need 80 assorted squares for the main portion of the quilt.

You will need 40 squares for the border.

It will be 10 squares **across**, including the border squares.

Use 8 assorted squares of fabric for each row, then add a border square on each side of the row. (Total of 10 squares per row.)

Use the border fabric to make a row of 10 squares. Make two of these rows, one for the top end of the quilt, and one for the bottom end of the quilt.

It will be 12 rows in **length**, including the border squares.

Sew the 10 rows together. Then sew the bottom and top border rows onto the ends of the quilt.

Use 1 to 2 yards of fabric to cut out enough material to attach to the back of the quilt. Fold over edges, all around, and pin. Then sew together.

~ *Joyful Living*~

"Blessed is the people that know the joyful sound: they shall walk, O Lord, in the light of thy countenance."

Psalm 89:15

"God be merciful unto us, and bless us; and cause his face to shine upon us; Selah."

Psalm 67:1

"Trust in him at all times; ye people, pour out your heart before him: God is a refuge for us. Selah."

Psalm 62:8

"Wait on the Lord: be of good courage, and he shall strengthen thine heart: wait, I say, on the Lord."

Psalm 27:14

~ ~ ~ ~ ~ ~ ~

I hope you find these charts helpful. Be sure to adjust them to meet your own household needs. The goal is to have a pleasant home with a faithful house- keeper who enjoys her work.

I once read something in an old Grace Livingston Hill novel about the lady of the house giving directions to her maid. She mentioned that company would be arriving soon and to be sure the house was in order. The maid responded with something like, "The house is always in order." May that be our cheerful motto - to do our best work each day and to always have the house in order.

~ ~ ~ ~ ~ ~ ~

~ *Take Time to Be Holy*~

"Take time to be holy,

Speak oft with thy Lord;

Abide in Him always,

And feed on His Word.

Make friends of God's children;

Help those who are weak:

Forgetting in nothing

His blessing to seek."

Hymn by: William D. Longstaff, 1882.

The Blessing of Home

THE FOUR SEASONS OF LIFE: OLD AGE.

Bless this house

Oh Lord we pray,

Keep it safe

By night and day.

~ ~ ~ ~ ~ ~ ~ ~

113

~THE END ~

{Illustration on previous page: "The Four Seasons of Life: Old Age," 1868 by Currier and Ives.}

About the Author

Mrs. White has been a housewife for more than 30 years. She is the granddaughter of a revival preacher, Mother of 5, and a grandmother of 12.

She has been writing about homemaking on her blog, "The Legacy of Home" since 2009.

She lives with her family in an old 1800's house in rural Vermont.

Please visit Mrs. White's blog:

https://thelegacyofhome.blogspot.com

For more titles by The Legacy of Home Press, please visit us at:

https://thelegacyofhomepress.blogspot.com

Made in the USA
Las Vegas, NV
22 December 2023

83361382R00066